MW01248455

there has always
been magic within
me

winnie kendrick

there has always been magic within me

by winnie kendrick

winnie kendrick

Winnie's Window Co, LLC
Fort Worth, TX | https://msha.ke/winniekendrick

First edition: July 2024

Identifiers: LCCN: XXXXXXXXXX | ISBN: XXX-X-XXXXX-XXX-X (hardback) ISBN: XXX-X-XXXXX-XXX-X (paperback) | ISBN: XXX-X-XXXXX-XXX-X (ebook)

there has always been magic within me

for my darling girl,
for my inner child,
for every cursebreaker –

you are made of magic.

winnie kendrick

there has always been magic within me

contents

winnie kendrick

there has always been magic within me

the hunt

winnie kendrick

cursed

there is poison within me,
put there by the only person
who was supposed to
love me
comfort me
love me
i said that already, didn't i?
it's hard to remember sometimes
with the darkness looming in every corner,
every crevice, of my mind.
my words are venomous, my mind a snare,
watching, waiting, observing, strategizing.
what will keep me safe?
what will cause me harm?
which am i more afraid of?
be careful, i learned how to wield
my sharp tongue from the very best.
mothers have been loving their daughters for centuries.
mothers have been hating their daughters for centuries.
i must be cursed, to deserve your hatred.
my therapist asked me what my worst
self-delusion is,
and i told her "that i'm a bad person, and i've tricked everyone
into believing in my goodness."
what else am i supposed to think
when the woman who gave me life
constantly snuffed out my will to live,
while making everyone
distrust

dislike
devalue
me.

i'm not good.
i can't be.
i'm cursed.
but goddamn, do i try to be
better
kinder
softer
than i was ever taught.

when i learned i was having a daughter, i was
petrified.
what if i end up just like her?
but...
i love her.
i love her so much, sometimes it feels my heart will never be big
enough to give her
all of the love she deserves.
and she is so small but already so much
softer
kinder
better
than i can ever hope to be.

my friend has me saved in her phone under
"cursebreaker"
because i have the potential for
staying cursed
or

becoming magic
and my daughter was made
of stardust, and love, and magic.
so, i will break this curse,
so that my daughter won't have to.

forgiveness

i can't forgive you.
when i was a child, i used to think
that one day i would wake up and you would
change.
like a fairy tale.
you would apologize for everything,
be the mother i always dreamed about,
wished for.
i didn't realize
that that apology wouldn't come
until i was 24, and had become a mother myself.
and that's why i cannot forgive you.
because i know firsthand
just how fucking easy it is to show my daughter
unconditional
love.
so while you made it a point to
trap me
paralyze me
traumatize me,
i make it a point to tell my daughter that i love her
always;
when she's happy
when she's sad
when she's mad.
my favorite sound in the whole world is the sound
of my daughter's belly laugh.
your favorite sound
must've been the way my voice caught

as i choked on sobs
caused by some casual cruelty that you
decided to deal out that day.

because it was a decision.
to hate me the way you did was a
conscious
effort.

it's taken me a while to understand
why i can never forgive you.
or anyone, really.
i don't have it in me.
how can you forgive someone
when the only kindness they've shown you
is keeping their hands off of you,
yet brutalizing you in
every
other
way?
so, no.
i can't forgive you.
not for you, and not for me.

you could've chosen to love me
you could've chosen kindness
you could've chosen empathy
you could've chosen understanding
you could've chosen to love me
and yet
you
didn't.

so now i'm choosing
not to forgive you.
or anyone.

except for her.
the most beautiful person in this world,

with so much kindness in her tiny body it
overwhelms me.

i have strength in knowing that
despite my predispositions for
cruelty
coldness
hatred...
that i am raising a little girl full of
compassion
kindness
love.

forgiving her will be as easy as loving her,
because it isn't a choice i have to make.
loving her is easier than breathing.
holding her when she cries is harder than i expected,
because all i want is to take her pain away,
see her smile and giggle again.

so no,
i wont forgive you,
i wont let you get away with the bullshit
"i did the best i could!"

i
don't
care.

they say the path to hell was paved with good intentions.

but do you think
as abraham's hand shook as he
held the knife to sacrifice his son,
do you think isaac cared
when the story was retold?

do you think isaac empathized with his father,
whose decision was "impossible"?

or do you think,
maybe isaac was horrified
because what kind of a child
deserves to feel unsafe around the person
they trusted,
they believed in,
more than anyone? more than any god?

i don't think isaac forgave abraham.
i don't think i'll forgive you.

identity crisis

i want to carve out
the parts of you
in me.
the mangled, rotting piece of my heart
the cavernous, echoey trap of my mind
the bleeding parts of my soul.
i've had that desire ever since i could remember.
maybe that was why,
blades never felt safe in my hands.
maybe that was why,
i relished in the sight of my own blood.
maybe that was why,
i always wanted to
burn myself,
disappear,
and rise from the ashes anew.

maybe i was never trying to kill myself.
maybe i was trying to kill the pieces of you,
the pieces that rot and decay and demolish.
the memories of your words,
your actions,
inactions.

i remember sobbing to my lover once,
that i hate how much i hate me.
that i hate how i have to learn to love myself,
because i was never taught.
to love should be as natural as

breathing.
how could you not have taught me?
and you can't say

"i didn't love myself"
because i still don't love myself,
and my daughter knows only my love.

when my daughter was born,
i always thought
she would be better off without me.
because i came from you,
and you poisoned me,
so surely, i would poison her.
but,
slowly,
i realized that we are not the same.
i realized that i would rather die
than make my daughter feel
anything
close
to what you made me feel.
i realized that,
when i was a little girl,
and all i wanted to be was someone's mama,
it was because,
childishly,
i figured, if i couldn't get what i wanted,
what i needed,
(for you to be a real fucking mother)
i would become that for myself.

you didn't have room for me, in your life,
in your heart.

it's never been about me, has it?
it's always
been
you.

just the way you need it to be.

i didn't hate myself,
i didn't want to kill myself,

it's always
been
    y
      o
        u

evil witch

i only ever wanted
to be woken up
with a smile,
to the smell of waffles.

i didn't want extravagant trips to
nowhere.
i didn't want fancy clothes, or shoes, or toys.
i only ever wanted
love
gentleness
smiles
hugs
~~you~~.

the worst part is,
i know all of your smiles (though few) were forced.
i know all of your hugs (somehow fewer) were stiff.
on purpose, or not, it doesn't matter.

how could you have hated me so much,
to not show me any kind of
affection?
were you that
embarrassed
ashamed
angry
with me?

could you not risk
to be reminded of your greatest mistake
by showing it any emotion?

it's okay, i don't want your pity.
what i want is
accountability.
because how is it
that you hated me
and forced me to wake you up
to drive me to school--
(and you always made me late)
(and you never packed me lunch)
(and you never gave me a real 'i love you')
(and you always put me into fight or flight or survival mode)--
and yet,
i,
who in your eyes
(and the eyes of all those who listen to your tales)
i am the great
the terrible
the cursed
the wretched
the abusive
the manipulative
the evil
witch...

but, this evil witch
can still get up
and make waffles
for my daughter in the mornings.

this evil witch
loves to smile at her daughter,
and see her smile in return.

this evil witch loves her daughter,
so what does that make you?

bedtime story

once upon a time,
there was a little princess.
a princess who believed in
dancing in soft grass,
giggling without restraint,
smiling without composure,
and she was
happy.

the little princess had a father,
who was younger than he should've been,
but he still loved his little princess.
he spun her around as they danced in the grass,
he told stories to hear her lilting giggle,
he did anything to see her smile.
he may not have been the best king,
(how could he be? he was so young)
but he
tried,
he always tried.

the young king had a wife,
a chameleon in human skin,
with a venomous tongue
and wretched mind.
one day,
after a long journey alone,
leaving his wife in charge of their daughter,
the young king noticed,

that his little princess was
nervous
anxious

terrified.

"you're shaking, my flower," he said to her.
but, the little princess was too small,
too small to tell him,
too small to express the sheer
dread
terror
confusion
that now clouded her small heart.
she only held onto him,
with her tiny hands clenched into fists.
and the king knew,
he had to free her,
they had to escape.

and so, he notified the castle,
but by the time he went,
to quietly sneak his little princess away,
she was
gone.
and so was her mother.

panicked, the young king went in search of
his little princess.
and it took some time, but when he saw her,
he didn't think,
he just

took her,
to free her,
to save her,
to see her smile again.

but the mother, the evilest of queens,
snatched the little princess back,

threatening the king with an impossible decision,
his life, or the little princess'.
he fought, but in the end
the evil queen won.

the young king, never stopped trying,
but the little princess' mind was being
poisoned
confused
against him
until she could no longer recall
how much she did love her father.
all that was left,
was anger.

the little princess no longer danced.
the little princess no longer giggled, not without doubting
herself,
never fully
trusting
herself
anymore.
and the little princess now only smiled,
after practicing in the mirror.

and so, the little princess lived
unhappily ever after,
until she ran away from the evil queen.
and built herself up,
slowly putting the pieces back together,
stumbling and falling along the way,
but she was trying.
she was always trying.

and one day,

after she met her own dashing, handsome prince,
and they had a little princess of their own,
she found the king again.
he was older now,
and she did not recognize him,
or remember the times they had together.
but as she watched him play with her little princess,
she liked to think
that that was how she was like
with him.
as she watched her prince play with their daughter,
she liked to think
that that was how she had been, once:
wild,
carefree,
happy.

the thing they don't tell you about
fairytales,
is just how horrific it feels
up until the

happily
ever
after.

with the self destruction inside me,
put there by the evil queen,
i fear i will never
be
happy.
i fear i will never let myself.

but, like the young king,
i will never stop trying,
because my little princess deserves to be happy.

and maybe,
just maybe,
that means that i deserve to be happy, too.

intruder

maybe i did deserve it.
maybe i am
just as bad
as i was always told.
maybe i was not made for
love
peace
happiness.
maybe i was born from
hatred
and loathing
and ugliness.
maybe that's all i was destined for.
maybe i can never be happy.
maybe i have always been and will always be
my mother's cursed daughter.
maybe everything i touch wilts
(*stop*)
maybe i destroy everything i love
(*wait*)
maybe i am going to be
(*don't*)
just
(*please*)
like
her
(*NO!*)

do you know how exhausting it is
to be at war with your own mind?

to be the villain in your own story?

maybe this is why i wish for
silence.
maybe this is why i can never
look someone in the eyes for too long
because if you look too closely,
you'll see.
you'll see what i see.
a monster
a witch
a poison.
maybe this is why i can't stand the sight of me.

but
somewhere,
down deep in the caverns of my blackened soul
i know this is not true.

but even still,
like a wish, in the dead of night,
you might hear me whisper,
like a woman possessed,
'i am good, i am good, i am good'
'i am not her, i am not her, i am not her'
'i am not cursed, i am not cursed, i am not cursed'
'i will be better, or i will die trying'

but right now,
my daughter is playing with her toy cars
and she looks so beautiful with the sunlight streaming in,
and i don't have time to be my own intruder.

mirror

i wonder if my daughter will ever see
the cracks in this mask.
i wonder if,
when playing hide and seek,
i will shout 'boo!'
and she will freeze
in horror.
i wonder if
one day
she will see.
see the ugly, marred skin,
leathery to the touch.
see the imperfect blemishes,
the crazed look in my eyes.
see the monster that is within me.
that has always been within me.

i hope she won't.
i hope she will only ever see
that her mama wants to make her smile,
and chase her
not because i love the hunt,
but because she loves to run.

i don't think she will.
because she kisses me,
and she doesn't recoil.
she smiles and giggles and runs

wild,
wild like i long to be,
and she is beautiful.
she is brilliant.
she is perfect.

maybe i am not a reflection of my mother,
maybe i am a reflection of *her*,
my beautiful baby girl.
maybe i can stop
wincing
whenever i see myself in the mirror,
breaking apart my skin,
to draw blood,
because surely, monsters don't bleed
(at least not by my weak hand).

but maybe...
i'm not a monster.
maybe it was all a lie--
a projection from someone who,
instead of telling me
what a monster i was,
should have told me that i was
beautiful
and brilliant
and perfect
too.

maybe i can try,
just try,
to look at myself with

a kindness i was never shown,
but that i learned
quickly and
easily
for my daughter.

to see a beauty in me that
others
tell me i possess.

to see that
my daughter
was made of
magic and
stardust and
beauty.

to see that
my daughter
was born from
me,
and that must mean
i am not as
monstrous
as i was raised to believe.

until then though, i will play
hide and seek with my daughter,
and avoid my mirror.

winnie kendrick

there has always been magic within me

the trial

winnie kendrick

complicated

you didn't love me.
i don't love me.

but,
she loves me.

she who i created,
with the love and darkness and spite inside of me,
who is made of nothing but love and light and courage,
she loves me.

and i think,
no.
i know that's enough.

i never needed your love,
with its conditions and shards of glass.

i only ever needed to survive
you
so that i could meet
her.

she is better than you.
she is better than me.

she loves me.
and by the gods,
i am trying to love me, too.

not for you.
not for me.

but,
for her.

always for her.

happy birthday

"you're okay,"
i whisper to you,
in a hushed, repeated prayer,
even if i wasn't,
even if i was terrified,
even if
your tiny body in my arms
on my chest
felt so fragile,
that i became so scared
immediately
that i would ruin you.

your tiny cries were so
refreshing,
because you will never know
just how much i
agonized
dreaded
feared
your safe arrival.

because,
i am cursed.
and every time
i have ever wanted something
even half as much
as i wanted you,

my self-destructive tendencies
or the universe
(though, i like to think the former)

seem to find a way
to catalyze
my
destruction.

i am not perfect,
and i knew,
from the second i knew about you,
that you were.
and i didn't know
how someone like me
would make someone like you.

but,
just as the bumblebees find their flowers,
to nestle into, to sleep,
and the sun chases the moon,
and the stars twinkle in the night sky,
i knew that we would be okay.

and so,
as you fought through the trauma,
of being brought into this life,
i held you close,
rubbed your back,
and i told you,
"you're okay,"
"you're safe,"
"we're okay."

and i still believe that.

as long as we have each other,
everything will be okay.

dear little me

i'm sorry.

i'm sorry to the wildness in me,
that i snuffed out,
because i had to be seen,
never heard,
to survive.

i'm sorry to the courageousness in me,
that was quickly replaced by
cowardice,
because i was too small
to fight the monster in front of me.

i'm sorry to the love in me,
that i spent years pouring into
a pot with no soil, and no seeds
only to find my water
kicked aside.

i'm sorry to the happiness in me,
that used to swell and bloom in my chest,
and made my smile rival the sun,
and my laugh bounce off of the trees,
and made me feel invincible.

i'm sorry to the love in me,
that used to push me,
to keep going

because surely,
surely, if i can love someone
who never loved me,

then maybe,
i can change them
then maybe,
i can save her.

i'm sorry to the sadness in me,
the once open and sunny fields of my mind,
turned into dark and cold and desolate streets,
paranoid of every sound,
and feeling like i deserve
every bad thing that could ever happen
to me.

i'm sorry to the anger in me,
put there by someone with nothing but hatred in their heart,
which makes my words venomous,
and my thoughts volatile,
towards everyone who has ever wronged me
(including myself).

i'm sorry to the forgiveness in me
i'm not sure
you actually existed.

i'm sorry to the violence in me
that i can only ever use
towards myself
in dark bathrooms
full of self-loathing.

i'm sorry to the gentleness in me,
that is now so
impossible
for me to fathom,
that i forget it was ever there.

i'm sorry to the anxiety in me,
second-guessing my every thought,
my every movement,
my every motive,
wholly distrusting of everything with
and without
a pulse
because if it can bleed,
or if it can't,
it can hurt you.

i'm sorry to the hope in me,
once so full,
now so empty,
from years of broken and empty
promises.

i'm sorry to me.

and i will do better,
for my daughter.

she will never lose her wildness,
her courageousness,
her love,
her happiness,
her gentleness.

i will never
be like
my mother.

if i could,
i would find
my smaller self,
and i would
hug her,
and tell her
how sorry i am
for how brave
and broken
she has to become.

but i would also tell her,
that there is beauty
in darkness
in survival.

and i would kiss her forehead,
wrap her in a warm blanket,
and let her cuddle with me,
because all she ever wanted
was to be held,
was to be loved.

through raising my daughters,

i can heal myself.

through loving my daughters,
i can learn to love myself,
to forgive myself
for everything i had to do
to survive.

through loving my daughters,
i can break the cycle.

witch trials

sometimes i like to think
that the tension in my neck,
the tightness in my chest,
is something i
earned,
like a badge of honor,
not learned
for my own survival.

sometimes i like to think
that there was magic in my lineage,
that my ancestors
were beautiful witches
who danced under the moon,
and wove flowers into one another's hair.

sometimes i like to think
that the rage in me
was put there by a legacy
of women before me.
women who suffered,
who endured,
who overcame.

and sometimes i wonder
if that tension in my neck,
is just a memory
from the noose
around theirs.

please don't call

i hate you.

i hate that
because of you
i hate me, too.

i hate that i have to learn
how to try to love me
because you never did.

i hate that i have to learn
how to not hate myself
because that's all you ever did.

i hate how sick i am,
to have genuinely thought,
that my daughter would be better off
without me
in this world.

i hate how tight my throat feels
when i remember clutching my phone
and the operator telling me,
"you're a great mother"
and i wanted so badly to believe her
but
couldn't.

i hate how the tears sting in my eyes

to remember that night,
the one where my hands shook
as i held the car keys

and the only words i could hear
were
yours.

i hate that i still feel unworthy
of this life that i have fought
so hard to create, to make my own.

i hate that all i ever wanted
was to be hugged,
and have you stroke my hair,
and take me out into the world,
and laugh with me,
unreservedly.

i hate that you were damaged, too.
by a loveless, careless home,
from a generation who
collapsed more than just the economy.

i hate that you let that define you.

i hate that you
never tried
to get better
until it was far too late.

i hate that i'm turning
far too serious an age
in less than a month.

my friend made a joke,

"25 sucks. your brain is stuck now."

and gods above,
do i hope that's not true.

because i still have
so much to
learn
and
unlearn.

so many curses to
break
and
banish.

so much more magic
to discover.

i hate my birthday,

because i know
(and you know, though you
refuse to admit it)
that my birth
marked the end
of your life.

i hate that you can't acknowledge that.
i hate that you can't accept that.
i hate that you still blame me,
when i never asked for this.

i hate that i have made peace
with my apathy for you.

i hate that i will never
get to just call my mom
and talk about life
or nothing
or both.

i hate that all i have
is my daughter
and the knowledge—
the cold and irrefutable truth—
that she will
never
know
this
hatred.

i hate my birthday,
and i hate you, too.

the gifts you gave me

apologies fall on my ears
like snow falls upon grass--
heavy and
deadly.

empty promises force
a ghost of a smile
on my lips.

i was trained to be polite.
i was trained to smile--
but not too wide,
it'd be a shame
if others saw your crooked teeth,
wouldn't it, dear?

sincerity makes my skin crawl
because all i ever knew
was synthetic, cold, performative
"love"
if you can call it that.

anger seems to be
the only thing
i fully inherited from
you.
an anger so strong,
so insurmountable,

i have often prayed,
to die
just for a moment

so i may come back
without this anger
that sits in my chest
like a weight i can never lift.

my anger comes out
lashing and snarling and cruel
at even those i hold most dear.

perhaps i am afraid,
when things get too comfortable,
that everyone i love will leave me
will see the ugly
the darkness
in me.
so i push,
and i claw,
and i scratch.

i don't mean to ruin everything i touch,
i never have.

but now,
now that i have her,
i have to confront
all of the ugly and dark parts of me.
i have to dissect
which parts i put there,
versus the parts that were taught to me.

i have to apologize
when i am wrong
i have to teach her how to apologize
while still encouraging her wildness.

i have to keep my promises
because she has to know
with absolute certainty
that she can always trust me.
i have to be sincere,
and accept sincerity in return,
because i will raise her to live
a life full of sincere love
and happiness
and beauty.

i have to control my anger
because my anger is not mine entirely.
it's yours.
it's yours and i don't want it anymore.
i will not pass this anger onto her
but it still makes my voice tremble,
and my hands shake.

one day
i will turn my anger into strength
and i will teach my daughter to do the same.

there has always been magic within me

the burning

55

winnie kendrick

choosing evils

when i was younger,
i never thought i would live this long.
i didn't see how i could,
being trapped in the way
only you could keep me.

i don't know how i survived.
i think i was too scared
of giving up my entire life
and letting you have
that last kind of control.

maybe it was fear,
maybe it was spite,
maybe those two things
aren't so different.

instead of dying,
i sacrificed myself,
to escape you.
to endure unending horror,
that my therapists now label --
complex post traumatic stress disorder, they say,
with a wounded look on their face
and all i can do
is grit my teeth
and smile
just like i was taught.

i didn't die

but often
i wished i had.

it's funny,

how different pain
catastrophizes you
in different ways.

i still wake up,
when someone creeps into the room,
with a gasp tearing from my throat,
the remnants of a trauma i cannot remember,
and am
terrified to rediscover.

but,
even with my broken pieces,
my broken mind,
i am here.

i am here.
i am able to hold my daughter,
rock her in my arms,
and read her
bedtime stories.

and that alone
makes me look back at my younger self,
with kinder eyes and say,

"you are alive, sweetheart."
"you are loved."
"you are okay."

and okay is good enough for now.

old wishing well

i wish i could believe
that the magic within me
is enough.

i wish that my magic
was all i needed
to break this curse.

i wish i could believe
in my own strength,
my powers.

i wish my heart
could find strength
in its anger, its sadness.

i wish i could believe
when my daughter says
"i love you more."

i wish my mind
would stop trying to convince me
(in a voice not my own)
that i am the monster.

i wish i could believe
in a beauty i possess
but cannot see.

i wish my flaws
were not the only thing i see
when i stare into the mirror too long.

i wish i could believe
that i am strong enough
to break this curse.

this curse of
obligatory love and
suffering and
anger and
sadness and
longing for something
(someone)
just within your reach
but they take your hands
and hold them over fire
until you are screaming
begging for them to stop
please, stop, please—

even if i'm not strong enough,
this curse will end with me.

i wish i could believe
in the magic within me.

reading with a ghost

one day,
when i am gone,
i hope that my daughter
can leaf through the pages
of the books i lost
and found
myself in.

i hope that she will--
with no sadness,
or regret,
or remorse,
(and please gods, no hatred)--
be able to read the stories
that gave me a sense of
hope and
belonging
when i felt lost.

i hope she will run her finger
beneath my annotations
and hear my voice
as she reads through them.

i hope she never feels alone,
and that perhaps,
through my books,
through the lives i lived
when my life was just unfolding,
i hope she can feel me with her.

because i believe,
with as much love as i poured into
the pages of greek tragedies,
romcoms,
fantasy,
i think it's fair to say
that a piece of me lives
somewhere in the binding.

i hope,
on hard days,
my children will find solace and
comfort
in those stories.

and i hope that
they will be able to feel my arms
wrapped around their shoulders,
holding them close,
like when they were oh so small.

i hope that my library
will be as magical for them
as it has been for me.

universe's daughter

i am made of the universe
i am made of pure love
and joy
and wildness.

i have starlight in my veins
and thunderstorms in my eyes.
i am beauty
and chaos
and strength
and pain
all at once.

i have a childish hope

somewhere, nestled deep inside of me,
where a small version of me,
holds a small, dim lit candle
inside of my soul.

(i think she is somewhere close,
i think she is nestled in my chest,
where my daughter rests her head)

i am capable of gentleness,
and violence.
my words can soothe,
like a calming balm,
or they can destroy,
and wreak a carnage on my world
that i can never heal from.

i have centuries of magic in my blood,
because isn't it so magical
to choose yourself
over
and
over again
in spite of everything?

i can feel the moon
kiss my cheek
as i gaze upon the stars,
whose very light
and dust
lives within me.

i can feel the forest
welcome me with open arms
to explore
to discover
to rest.

i can feel the warm embrace
of all that is,
all that isn't,
and the light and shadows
in between

this love, this raw energy
that surrounds me,
wrapping around my shoulders
like a soft blanket—

i found this.
in my darkest hours,

i discovered
that i am not just the unfortunate child
born to a plagued mother.

i discovered
the tiny bits and pieces
that the universe gifted to me.

i learned that the universe
became the mother i
always
needed.

she made sure
that my tiny heart
never lost its love.

and for that,
i am eternally indebted.

which is why i sit,
talking to the moon,
thanking the budding flowers,
becoming one with
every beautiful thing around me.

i bring out my evening coffee,
and i sit in the grass,
gazing upon the stars,
with the softest smile on my lips.

"*thank you*," i whisper,
and the gentle wind in my hair
tells me the universe thanks me, too.

for listening.
for enduring.

for having courage,
despite everything,
to bring another beautiful and magical life
into this world.

for keeping my daughter's childish
love, and joy, and wildness
alive.

for staying soft,
in a world like this.

inheritance

the hardest part of parenthood
is seeing your child—
so small, so sweet, so precious—
and having to realize
that you were like that
too.

raising my daughter
has been so healing
because i show myself
every day
that i am not
fated to become
evil and cruel
like my mother.

gods, do i know i have it in me.
the potential for
an evil so dark
so angry
it terrifies me.

it lives in me—
people speak of
"inner demons"
but i don't think they meant this.

i don't even know
whose evil it is anymore.

is it mine?
is it yours?

i don't know.

but i can always feel it—
i felt it when my daughter
was just a newborn
and i felt more love in my heart
than i ever had before—
but that darkness was still there
pulsing
pounding
demanding to be seen.

i had to use
all of the power within me
to fight against it.

when i feel my heart pounding,
and that angry evil building up,
threatening to tear through my mouth,
break my jaw,
and devour everything i love dear—

i have to
stop.
i have to
breathe.
i have to
fight.

every second of every day,
i have to fight.

when my daughter,
starts to show me
just the smallest sign

of that anger
(that i know i put in her)
instead of lashing back,
i tell her,
i remember to always tell her:

"i love you."
"i love you when you're happy."
"i love you when you're mad."
"i love you when you're sad."

my own little spell,
to ensure,
that she knows
above all else
that she is loved
unconditionally
by
me.

she needs to keep this strength,
this boldness.

this world was not made for her,
with its claws and teeth and dripping blood,

but she was made
of the universe
she was made
from me

and like me,
she will stop,
close her eyes,
breathe out,
and fight.

because i will teach her.
i will protect her
from me
from my mother
from her mother
from every unfortunate,
cursed mother
in my rotted family tree.

she will be
free.
she will never know
that she was the daughter
of a cursed woman
because i will break my bones
i will tear out every dark piece of me
i will rip out
my own beating heart
to free her.

to raise her with love,
and light,
and music,
and sunflower fields,
and pumpkin patches,
and meadows,
and kindness.

i can do this.
i have no other choice.

if i could talk to my mother in 1998

can i tell you a secret?
a terrible,
horrible,
harrowing secret?

lean in close,
because i will not repeat this--
it's a terrible thing,
this secret.

in a hushed tone i will tell you,
beneath a sky
where the clouds are hiding the moon
because i cannot bear
to say this under glorious moonlight.

are you ready?

...

i get it.

i understand how impossible it can feel
when your baby is screaming
and it's the worst sound in the world
and you wish
more than anything
that you had never been able to hear at all.

i understand the tension in your shoulders,
as you hold your tiny creation
and they're fighting you,

and you're exhausted,
and you grit your teeth,
and maybe you even raise your voice,
just a little.

i understand how overwhelming it feels
to always give your all to everyone else
until every single nerve ending is fried,
overstimulated,
and you have no energy for yourself.

i understand how conflicted you feel
having to love someone else—
your bleeding heart—
while having never been taught
how to love yourself.

i get it.

i get that it can feel like too much
all at once
everywhere
all the time.

it's hard to make mistakes,
it's hard to always apologize
when something sinister slips through the cracks
and you do raise your voice,

or you snap,
or you hide from your child, in a dark bathroom, with the vent
running, so you can have
just one goddamn moment
of quiet.

i know the guilt,

because you've wanted this forever,
you've wanted to be a mother,
to give someone else
the kind of love
you never got.

i know how unending your self-doubt feels,
because how did you expect yourself to love anyone,
when every time you tried to love
the one person
who should have loved you more,
you were
tossed
aside?

when all you know is darkness,
how did you think
you could bring light
into your world?

i know you're tired.
i know how hard you're fighting.
but do you know what else i know?

i know that you are strong.
i know that,
even in those moments,
where you question your worth,
where you convince yourself
that your child would be better off
with anyone else for a mother,
i know you have a goodness in your soul
that, though hidden,
shines brighter than the sun.

i know that your heart,
with its bandages and scars,
still pumps strong and steady
for your child.

i know that your love
is unending
and pure
and beautiful.

keep going.
i promise, though it feels impossible at times,
it's worth it.

please,
i know you have a hard time trusting people,
but you have to trust me.

your daughter
is the most beautiful person
to ever exist

because she is the only her that has ever been
and you should love her
because she didn't ask to be here.

if you don't listen to me,
and if you lean into every
horrible
terrible feeling?

you
will
lose
her.

so please,
listen to me.

acknowledge your sadness,
your anger,
your fear,
and learn to love yourself.

hold
yourself
accountable.

otherwise you will be
all alone
with no one to blame
but yourself.

and you will have to hear about your daughter
and her daughter

through flashes of photographs
that she sends to everyone
but
you.

hold
yourself
accountable.

cursebreaker

"i have to do this," i say
as i grit my teeth
and fight that darkness within me.

"i have to do this," i whimper
as i cover my ears with my hands
and block out those dangerous thoughts.

"i have to do this," i scream
until my throat goes raw and raspy
as i struggle against myself.

"i have to do this," i assert,
calmly, with an authority i do not believe in
despite the thunderstorm swelling up inside me.

"i have to do this," i sob,
as tears stream down my face
and doubt myself being able to.

"i have to do this," i whisper quietly,
my voice quivering in the safety of the moonlight,
but not breaking.

"i have to do this," i whisper softly,
as i hold her to my chest
and run my fingers through her hair.

"i have to do this," i grit out,
my teeth now bared
as i let my anger wash over me to defeat that darkness,
put in me by someone i cannot recognize anymore.

"i have to do this!" i shriek,
as my confidence grows
slowly, but surely.

"i hate that i have to do this," i cry,
into my lover's arms
as he holds me close to him,
letting my head rest upon his beating heart.

"you can do this," they tell me,
ny closest people, my own personal village,
when i confess how close i feel to giving up.

"you can't do this," they tell me,
hatred in their voices
their pitchforks aimed right at my home
when i draw my boundaries, when i finally
stand up
for myself.
but all they can think about
is protecting the evil woman that they created.
because it's easier,
so much easier,
to blame the thing--
the lying monster,
the evil witch,

the cursed daughter--
that ruined her life,
than to ever
force her
to confront herself.

"i have to do this," i tell myself,
through everything.

through the bad days,
where i am convinced
that i will be just like her anyways,
so what does it matter?

through the hard days,
where i react like she would
and hate myself that much more,
before i apologize to the ones i have hurt,
with a tongue so sharp and lethal,
i have to cut my own mouth
before i consider opening it to speak.

through the good days,
where my daughter is running and giggling
and playing and observing
and learning and growing and
teaching
me.

"i have to do this," i whisper softly,
as i think about everything i endured
for my daughter to be here

snuggled in my arms
as i read her a story.

"i love you more," my daughter tells me
with a bright smile and a confidence in her voice
that i am still trying to master.

"i love you more," my daughter tells me
when she can see i am
hurting,
despite my best efforts to hide it.

"i love you more," my daughter tells me
and that is everything
to me.

"i have to do this," i say,
no wavering or anger in my voice,
just raw conviction, devotion.

i will pay for the sins of my mother,
i will pay for the sins of her mother,
and the mothers before that,
who cursed my family tree.

i have to do this,
because it's what i was born for.

i
am
the
cursebreaker.

and i will see this through.
every heartwrenching moment
where i have to tear myself apart
inspect the pieces
and cut out the poison.
every blurry memory
blurred for my own protection
i will force up
because i have to confront
everything.
every dark crevice
will have a light shine down
so i can determine if these monsters,
are a raging anger

or a weeping, terrified child
who never got to heal.

this curse ends with me.

there is magic within me
for this very reason.

i
am
the
cursebreaker.

because my daughter deserves better.
because i deserved better.
because you deserved better.

this curse will end with me,

because it has to.

my daughter will never
feel the pain
i endured
from my own mother.

she will know she can
trust me
find safety with me
find comfort and love and security in me.
she will be happy,
happy like i never was.

she is my savior,
so small, she already protects me
from childish things,
but she stands in front of me
as if blocking me from the danger
of some thing i cannot see
that she can.

i am already breaking this curse.
i can see it in her happiness,
her strength,
her kindness.

i will break this generational curse
because this pain and heartbreak and suffering
has to end with me.

so i will recite my incantation,
"i have to do this,"

like a woman inspired by her madness,
by her convictions,
until it is ended.

and right now,
i have to grab my daughter from her room,
hold her close,
and listen as she babbles about everything and nothing,
and ask her what she wants for breakfast.

i will end this curse.

and so will you.

winnie kendrick

there has always been magic within me

the end is really just the beginning, isn't it?

winnie kendrick

acknowledgements

as always, first and foremost, i will never be able to thank my best friend, mara jade, enough for her support and love and encouragement while i spiral like a madwoman during the creation of these poetry collections. i love you to the square root of infinity and beyond.

to my darling girls, who have taught me so much and have, in their tiny, unknowing ways, helped me more than i can properly express on this healing journey of mine: i love you both to the moon and back again.

to my husband, who alone has taught me so much about the art of loving myself through the way he loves me: i love you most, always and forever.

and, of course, to you, dear reader. you who i do not know, yet am so infinitely proud of. you have have faced adversity and, like a phoenix, risen from the ashes. i see you, i am proud of you, i love you, and i thank you for sharing this journey with me.

winnie kendrick

about the author

as soon as she figured out how to properly hold a crayon in her hand, winnie began to write. as she grew older, writing became her only solace. words are the most powerful instrument in the world, and winne hopes to continue ger writing career for as long as she lives, to help possibly leave this world a better place than how she found it. she hopes to make beautiful creations while also making memories in her little farmhouse with her darling girls, her husband, and of course, her books.

find winnie online:
@authorwinniekendrick on Instagram or
email winniedrabbles@gmail.com

winnie kendrick

winnie's upcoming works:

girlhood ... 07. 2024

a confrontation of unhealed trauma with nothing but light, softness, romanticisms, and rediscovery

the madness of healing ... 10. 2024

what happens when the evil witch fights back against her cursed village

winnie kendrick

there has always been magic within me

winnie kendrick